# SOAP MAKING

*A Beginners Guide to Making Natural Herbal Handmade Organic Soaps from Scratch*

**Laruent Wygant**

© **2015**

Laurent Wygant is an award winning personal development expert. Since 1990, she has taught at Universities around the world and continues to spread her knowledge from continent to continent.

She loves to teach Yoga, Mudras and Chakras. As a certified instructor of 7 year, everyone can share her desire for tranquility and happiness.

Her other passions include: Natural Soap Making

Wygant is known for her revolutionary approach to difficult concepts and breaking them down to simple stages that anyone can digest and use.

She has a passion for sharing his expertise, written numerous bestselling books, loves to read and write and most of all helping people.

# INTRODUCTION

Thank you for purchasing Soap Making: Beginners Guide to Making Natural Herbal Handmade Organic Soaps from Scratch.

In this book we teach you the basics of Soap Making, equipment necessities, tried and true soap recipes, and how to make your own recipes.

We teach the essentials of:

- Soap And Safety
- What is Soap?
- Safety Measures
- Needed Equipment
- Soap Making Equipment:
- Specialty Items that will be very helpful in making your soap
- Utensils you will need
- Containers you will need
- Safety Equipment
- Odds and Ends
- The Steps To Making Soap
- Soap Recipes

- Natural Calendula Soap:
- Oats and Honey Soap:
- Lavender Soap:
- Herbal Soap:
- Creating Your Own Recipes
- Another way to look at your oils

We also discuss soap cooking safety and the hazards of working with lye.

We discuss the basics of mixing soap, molding soap, drying soap, and how long to expect soap to last.

We detail information about storing soap to make it stay fresh and clean.

We recommend you use older equipment that is still useful instead of buying expensive, shiny new implements. Many of the needed supplies will be on hand already and probably duplicated. It is very important that you use tempered glass or stainless steel products for handling lye. Lye is a corrosive and will melt plastic and have a chemical reaction with aluminum. Always use a wooden spoon, not a metal one.

- Soap making is a fun hobby that has double rewards:
- The creativity and imagination used in making it, and

- The usefulness of the completed product.

We hope you have many happy years practicing your new hobby of soap making.

# Copyright 2015 by Laruent Wygant - All rights reserved.

This document is geared towards providing exact and reliable information in regards to the topic and issue covered. The publication is sold with the idea that the publisher is not required to render accounting, officially permitted, or otherwise, qualified services. If advice is necessary, legal or professional, a practiced individual in the profession should be ordered.

From a Declaration of Principles which was accepted and approved equally by a Committee of the American Bar Association and a Committee of Publishers and Associations.

In no way is it legal to reproduce, duplicate, or transmit any part of this document in either electronic means or in printed format. Recording of this publication is strictly prohibited and any storage of this document is not allowed unless with written permission from the publisher. All rights reserved.

The information provided herein is stated to be truthful and consistent, in that any liability, in terms of inattention or otherwise, by any usage or abuse of any policies, processes, or directions contained within is the solitary and utter responsibility of the recipient reader. Under no circumstances will any legal responsibility or blame be held against the publisher for any reparation, damages, or monetary loss due to the information herein, either directly or indirectly.

Respective authors own all copyrights not held by the publisher.

The information herein is offered for informational purposes solely, and is universal as so. The presentation of the information is without contract or any type of guarantee assurance.

The trademarks that are used are without any consent, and the publication of the trademark is without permission or backing by the trademark owner. All trademarks and brands within this book are for clarifying purposes only and are the owned by the owners themselves, not affiliated with this document.

# Table of Contents

CHAPTER 1: SOAP AND SAFETY

CHAPTER 2: NEEDED EQUIPMENT

CHAPTER 3: THE STEPS TO MAKING SOAP

CHAPTER 4: SOAP RECIPES

CHAPTER 5: CREATING YOUR OWN RECIPES

CONCLUSION

# CHAPTER 1: SOAP AND SAFETY

**What is Soap?**

Soap is a compound used with water to wash and clean surfaces and skin. Soap is a combination of oils or fats with an alkali like sodium hydroxide, with the addition of essential oils or perfume and color added for attractiveness.

Soap has a very simple recipe for the needed ingredients:

1. Oil or rendered fat,
2. Lye, sometimes called sodium hydroxide crystals,
3. Distilled or purified water.

This is the purest form of soap you can make. It works beautifully, but has no scent and is not an attractive color. Adding essential oils, dried flowers, and coloring can add some zing to your homemade soaps.

Lye and oil are both chemical compounds. When two compounds combine in a chemical bond they make a third chemical compound, in this case, soap. The chemical bonding process when combining the lye and the fat and water will activate the lye to bond with the oil. This will eliminate the lye and create the soap.

A natural, herbal handmade organic soap will have less additives than a commercially prepared soap. You will want to select less chemicals and processed ingredients so that you can claim a fully organic product. We suggest that you use essential oils for an infusion of scent, dried herbs for an adornment, and spices to give it a more attractive color than cold animal fat. Your first few batches may not be the most esthetically pleasing, but they will be functional and you will be learning texture and soap making basics. After you have the process down pat then we will address the beautification of soaps.

**Safety Measures**

Wear safety goggles and rubber gloves while handling the lye to protect your skin and your eyes. Lye is caustic and can burn when you touch it. It will ruin garments so wear very old clothes that can be thrown away or a heavy apron that covers from neck to knees.

White vinegar is a neutralizer for lye. If you spill or splash the lye, pour white vinegar liberally over the lye, then rinse it with cold water.

When you are mixing the lye, pay attention to the texture of the lye crystals. It is dangerous to let them clump together. Large clumps of lye can explode if the lye is heated all at once. When combining lye and water, add lye to the water and not the other way around. This helps the lye to dissolve quicker and more evenly. Continually stir your lye/water mixture with a wooden spoon. Do not use a metal utensil for this portion of the recipe, only a wooden spoon. Lye gets hotter as it absorbs the water, be careful not to splash or stir too quickly as it will burn you two ways, a chemical burn and a temperature burn.

Oil is a determiner of the type of soap you will make. You can use fat, like lard or rendered beef fat, or you can use oil. Whichever you use, it must be used in the liquid state, so that it will blend uniformly. If you use oils, limit yourself to no more than three varieties. When you combine oils, it can change the texture to the soap to be more gentle. Mixing oils gives a very fine and unique texture to your results.

Water, the last foundational ingredient to soap making, should be distilled or purified. The water is what causes the chemical reaction with the lye to bond it to the oils or fats. Do not use liquid lye, only lye crystals. Your ingredients should be weighed and measured carefully.

When the water activates with the lye, the lye and oils turn to soap. The lye actually disappears. As the soap dries, it will also lose much of the water, and it will also shrink. This is part of the normal drying process.

# CHAPTER 2: NEEDED EQUIPMENT

The only materials safe to use when working with lye are those made from glass, Pyrex, polypropylene (PP), and stainless steel. Any other equipment, copper, aluminum or Teflon, etc., will have a chemical reaction with the lye and can be possibly explosive or corrosive.

All of your equipment can be purchased online or at a soap or hobby store. The more exclusive the store, the more expensive the equipment will be.

If you have duplicates of some of the materials listed, use them instead of buying new products. They will be just as useful and nowhere near as expensive. We also suggest that you shop at Thrift stores, Dollar stores, or Goodwill stores to find the most frugal way to manage your hobby.

**Soap Making Equipment:**

## Specialty Items that will be very helpful in making your soap

1. **Kitchen Scale**-Doesn't have to be high-dollar, but a reliable digital scale will make weighing your ingredients much more accurate. You will have better results with your soaps by being an exacting measurer. One ounce difference can be crucial when working with a chemical reaction.

2. **Digital Thermometer**-When mixing lye, water, and oil together, it's important for them to be in the same temperature range within a few degrees. You need an accurate and easy to read thermometer or you risk your ingredients not mixing properly and losing your batch of components.

3. **Stick or Immersion Blender**-These are highly recommended from experienced soap makers and likely the most expensive ingredients outside of essential oils. The immersion blender is necessary to get the ingredients to combine and come to the "trace" stage. I recommend trying any kind of second hand store and seeing if you can get a used one, just to save your budget.

4. **Molds**-Molds are containers in which you pour the trace liquid after mixing. These containers can be as simple as a wooden box frame, like a concrete frame, or as fancy as

impressioned plastic or silicon molds with designs stamped inside.

a. You will need containers to let your soap dry in for the first 24-48 hours; your soap will take on the shape of the containers. To be very frugal, you can also use silicon pans made for loaves of bread and make a loaf of soap instead.

b. After the first 24-48 hours you will take your semi-hard soap loaf and cut it into bars before completing the drying process. If you wait until the soap completely hardens you may find it very difficult to cut into bars.

**Utensils you will need**

- A stainless steel spoon-To mix your oils

- A large wooden long-handled spoon-To mix your lye water

- Stainless steel whisk-Good for really mixing in your essential oils, etc.

- Stainless steel strainer-Good for pouring your lye water through before adding it to your oils, it helps catch any lumps you may have.

- Silicone spatula-Good for scraping your soap mixture out of its mixing bowl and into the moulds.

**Containers you will need**

- Small containers for measuring oils, powders, etc.
- Deep stainless steel pan for heating up oils
- Container for measuring lye (Glass, Pyrex, PP)
- Container for measuring water and mixing in lye (Glass, Pyrex, PP)
- Stainless Steel mixing bowl
- You can also get pint and a quart canning jars to use for your containers. (We will use them in our basic recipe.)

**Safety Equipment**

- Goggles
- Gloves
- Smock or apron

**Odds and Ends**

- Newspaper
- An old towel

- Drying rack
- Plastic wrap

## CHAPTER 3: THE STEPS TO MAKING SOAP

These are the basic steps for soap making, also called the cold process. This recipe produces a good body and facial soap bar.

**Ingredients:**

1/4 cup Lye or 100% Sodium Hydroxide (they are the same thing)

3/4 cup cool water (Distilled or Purified water will give best results)

2/3 cup of olive oil

2/3 cup of coconut oil

2/3 cup of liquid oil of your choice (Grape seed oil, Sunflower oil, almond oil, or saffron oil are good options)

You'll notice these are measured out in standard measuring cups, these were figured out by converting measurements to make this first attempt at creating soap as easy as possible. You'll want to measure your oils in liquid form. There are some that tend to come in a solid form, especially rendered beef fat or lard. You have to warm them up a bit to liquify them for proper measurement. Note the lye will be in the crystallized form only.

**Protecting yourself and your work area**: You'll want to put on your protective equipment and cover your work surface with newspaper. Gather the items you'll need to create your soap so that everything is conveniently placed at your side. You'll want the towel, the canning jars, utensils for stirring, molds, the strainer, and containers for measuring ingredients. (Make sure you use a stainless steel measuring cup for the lye as it can melt certain plastics)

**Lye and Water**: In your quart jar you'll want to measure out your water, have your spoon ready, and then slowly add your lye as you mix. This is where your goggles will come in handy. You may even want to consider a mask to help cut down on the fumes that will start when you first combine your two ingredients. It will smoke for 30 seconds to a minute. Its best to make soap in a well ventilated area like your kitchen, where you can turn on your vent fan. Keep stirring as you add all your lye and continue stirring until it stops smoking and your water begins to clear. Once you've reached this point you can let your jar sit for a bit as you work on the next step. (Your lye water mixture will heat up during this process and will need some time to cool down)

**Heating your oil**: In your pint jar, you'll want to combine all your oils using your spoon to mix. Next put the whole jar in your microwave for about a minute. The oil will need to be heated to about 120 degrees, so be sure to check it. You can also immerse your jar in a pan of water for heating if you don't want to use a microwave. Once your oil has reached 120 degrees, it's good to go. Your Lye mixture should have cooled down to about 120 degrees as well. Now we wait, you need both to cool to somewhere between 105 and 95 degrees. If the temperature is much lower than this your soap will combine too quickly and you'll be left with a crumbly soap.

**Combining your ingredients**: When both your lye mixture and oils have cooled to the proper temperature you'll want to combine them. Try to make sure they are only a few degrees apart to get the best result with your soap. Add your oils to the mixing bowl; slowly add your lye mixture stirring constantly. (At this point is doesn't matter which spoon you use as were combining ingredients, but before this point it is a good idea to keep them separate, to avoid any early mixing of ingredients.) You'll want to mix by hand for at least 5 minutes before you change to a blender. Keep mixing until your soap has the same consistency as pudding, you may find that it lightens and it will become thick. There will be small lines or streaks in the batter. When it reaches this consistency it's considered to have reached "trace". Trace is the point when the oils and lye have fully mixed and are starting to combine to create your soap.

**Adding any extras**: If you want to add any herbs, essential oils for scent or any other additions like oatmeal, etc., now is the time to do it. Your whisk will really come in handy now for combining those ingredients. Remember that all coloring agents should be in a powdered form, even herbs and stems. They should have been completely dried for at least a year, to ensure that there is no moisture in the product, because it will cause your soaps to mold and rot. They will smell terrible, ruin the entire batch, and possibly contaminate other products you have in your storage area.

**Making your mold**: Lightly grease your soap molds with petroleum jelly so they will release the soap easily. Pour your mixture into your mold or molds and cover with plastic wrap. Wrap your molds into your towel to help keep the soap warm while your soap goes through saponification. This is the process where your ingredients will complete their transformation into soap and all your initial ingredients will be gone, combined to create our finished product.

**Drying it out**: Wait about 24 hours and check your soap. If it is still warm or soft let it sit for another 24 hours. It needs to be kept in a warm environment, maybe a Styrofoam cooler with the soap bars covered in both plastic wrap first, then aluminum foil for 48 hours. After this point, take away the extra insulation and leave it until it is cool and solid to the touch. Once it's cool you'll want to turn your mold out onto a piece of parchment paper or some kind of rack to continue curing. If you used a bread pan and created a "loaf" of soap I would recommend cutting it now. If you want till after the next step it could be extremely hard to cut into bars. Allow your soap to dry for another 4 weeks, if you're not using a drying rack you'll want to turn your soap once a week to make sure all sides get exposed to the air.

**Storing**: Once your soap is fully cured you'll need to store it properly for best results. You'll want to keep it in an airtight container or wrap it in waxed paper; homemade soap is a magnet for dust; to keep it fresh stores it properly. Essentially home made soap creates its own glycerin (a humectant), which pulls moisture from the air and that moisture is what attracts dust to it.

**Cleaning up**: The first step to cleaning up; any equipment or containers that were exposed to lye should be neutralized in white vinegar. Once you've used the vinegar you can wash your things like you normally would with soap and water. For everything else, the mixing bowl, etc., that are coated with residual lye and fat mixtures, instead of scrubbing for hours trying to get that oil off and risking burning yourself on any residual lye, I recommend leaving it be. Stick it in a garbage bag or set it out of the way somewhere, then in about a week wash it. Now instead of fighting and scrubbing nasty fat and lye you'll have things coated in soap! All you'll need to do to clean is soak your equipment in hot water and run a scrub pad over the surface. Your hands and elbows are saved.

**Handmilled Soaps**: Handmilled soaps are soaps that are made without the addition of lye as an ingredient. Technically, lye is an ingredient because all soap has a caustic agent. For your recipe purposes, you won't be handling lye. What you will be handling is shaved baby soap, like Ivory, or Fels-Naptha, a mild white soap. You will shave this soap with a knife or a grater into a bowl. You should combine 2 cups of shaved soap to one cup of water. Heat this either in a double boiler on top of the stove, or in the grated soap bowl in the microwave. Be careful not to get the soap too hot. Stir the ingredients very gently to combine them. If you stir too heartily you will bubbles that are impossible to remove. Lightly grease your soap molds with petroleum jelly so they will release the soap easily. Pour the soap into the mold and place in the refrigerator to set. Leave it overnight. Take the mold out of the refrigerator and turn out the bars. Cut them as desired and then leave to cure and dry for at least 3 weeks. Be sure to cover them so as not to attract dust.

# CHAPTER 4: SOAP RECIPES

** Please note these recipes will be in grams instead of the easy to follow cup measurements we used above, so this is where your scale will come in handy. Don't forget to zero your scale with the empty container before you weigh your ingredients to get the best results.

**Natural Calendula Soap:**

Makes a 1 lb. batch about 4-5 bars.

- 120 g of Water
- 64 g of Lye
- 1 tsp of dried Calendula Petals
- 112 g of Coconut Oil
- 164 g of Olive Oil

- 82 g of Palm or Tallow Oil
- 78 g of Sunflower Oil
- 19 g of Shea Butter
- 6 drops of antioxidant of your choice

For optimum results you should infuse your petals into your water by boiling water first and then adding the petals, allowing the mixture to cool before you use water. Lightly grease your soap molds with petroleum jelly so they will release the soap easily. Pour into the soap molds and let cure for 48 hours. Take out of the molds and cut as desired. Wrap and store for one month to cure and dry.

**Oats and Honey Soap:**

Makes a 1 lb. batch about 4-5 bars

- 120 g of Water
- 63 g of Lye
- 195 g of Olive Oil
- 136 g of Coconut Oil
- 68 g of Castor Oil
- 45 g of Palm or Tallow Oil
- 9 g of Beeswax
- 1 tsp of Honey (7 g)

- 1 tsp of Rolled Oats (2 g)
- 6 Drops of Antioxidant

You'll want to add the honey when your mixture just starts to begin to trace, and use a whisk to combine well. Next you'll add your oats, when your mixture hasn't quite reached full trace. Lightly grease your soap molds with petroleum jelly so they will release the soap easily. Pour into the soap molds and let cure for 48 hours. Take out of the molds and cut as desired. Wrap and store for one month to cure and dry.

**Lavender Soap:**

- Makes a 1 lb. batch about 4-5 bars
- 120 g of Water
- 64 g of Lye
- 164 g of Olive Oil
- 112 g of Coconut Oil
- 82 g of Palm or Tallow Oil
- 78 g of Sunflower Oil
- 19 g of Shea Butter
- 10g about a teaspoon of Lavender Essential Oil

- 1/4 tsp of mineral color (Ultramarine Violet) (optional)
- 1/2 tsp of dried lavender buds preferably chopped (optional)
- 6 Drops of antioxidant

Separate your mineral color and add small amounts of it to your different oils before you begin, mix well. Add your essential oil and lavender buds just before your soap reaches full trace. Lightly grease your soap molds with petroleum jelly so they will release the soap easily. Pour into the soap molds and let cure for 48 hours. Take out of the molds and cut as desired. Wrap and store for one month to cure and dry.

**Herbal Soap:**

- Makes a 1 lb. batch about 4-5 bars
- 120 g of Water
- 62 g of Lye
- 204 g of Olive Oil
- 136 g of Coconut Oil
- 91 g of Sunflower Oil
- 23 g of Shea Butter

- 10 g of Essential oil, basically a teaspoons worth, I would go for ones that match or compliment the dried herbs you'll use.

- 1 tsp of Dried Herbs, whatever you like there's lots of options out there. You can use just one or a few that compliment one another.

- 6 drops of Antioxidants

You'll want to boil the water first and infuse it with your dried herbs. Allow to completely cool before using. You'll add your essential oils to the mixture when your soap hasn't quite reached full trace. Lightly grease your soap molds with petroleum jelly so they will release the soap easily. Pour into the soap molds and let cure for 48 hours. Take out of the molds and cut as desired. Wrap and store for one month to cure and dry.

# CHAPTER 5: CREATING YOUR OWN RECIPES

Lastly, we will talk about the wide variety of ingredients you can use in your soaps and what they will add to the outcome. With this general knowledge you'll be able to move forward towards trying out your own recipes.

**Oils -** You can use any oil or fat to create soap, just remember each type will give your bar a different consistency or lather.

**Beeswax-**This will add a really nice scent to your soap, as well as help to make it hard, but you'll want to keep it to small amounts. If you use large amounts it will keep your soap from lathering.

**Coconut Oil-**Gives you a really fluffy lather for your soap, as well as being super cleansing, helps give you a hard soap.

**Olive Oil**-makes soap that is great for all skin types, and conditioning for the skin.

**Palm Oil-**Is great for soap making but it is recommend to make sure you find a product that is sustainable, so as to not continue the damage to protected animals habitats.

**Soybean Oil-**Provides great conditioning in your bar and a nice consistent lather.

Another way to look at your oils:

**Oils that create hard bars-**Beeswax, Coconut oil, Lanolin, Lard, Shea Butter, Tallow, Palm Oil

**Oils that cleanse-**Sunflower oil, Coconut oil, Palm Kernel oil

**Oils that produce a good lather-**Canola oil, cocoa butter, Hemp Seed oil and Jojoba oil all give a creamy lather. Coconut oil, Castor oil, Palm kernel oil all gives a fluffy lather.

**Oils that condition**-Avocado oil, Castor oil, Cocoa Butter, Apricot Kernel oil, Corn oil, Grape seed oil, Jojoba, Hempseed oil, Mango butter, Olive oil, Rice Bran Oil, Shea butter, and sweet almond oil.

Please note Jojoba, Apricot kernel oil, Avocado oil, Mango butter and the others listed below are meant for superfatting so please use accordingly.

**SuperFatting Oil**: You'll want to use these oils in smaller amounts. You'll add it at the very end of your soap making process, leaving it free floating. This will keep it from being transformed into soap when combined with the lye and impart more moisture to your finished product.

**Shea Butter-**Is best used as a superfatting oil due the difficulty it has with turning into soap. Though often times, even if added in the beginning of the process, it will stay a moisturizing butter instead of turning into soap.

**Cocoa Butter-**Provides great moisture for your skin, as well as providing good skin protection, will also help to harden your soap. Can be used as a regular oil but works better as a superfatting oil.

**Sweet Almond Oil-**Good because it leaves a light feeling and it can condition and moisturize your skin.

**Antioxidants:** We use these in soap like preservatives. You want to use preservatives in things that are wet because the moisture is a perfect environment for bacteria to grow. In basic soap the water will evaporate and we don't have to worry about using preservatives. When we use the superfatting method with certain oils they won't dry out and we risk getting rancid soap. We use these natural preservatives because they help any free floating oils stay stable and keep them from turning our beautiful soap into something totally gross.

- Grapefruit Seed Extract-It is extracted from the seeds and pulp of a grapefruit. It's a clear thick liquid that works great at keeping your soap from spoiling and doesn't add any unwanted scents.

- Rosemary Oleoresin Extract-This strong smelling liquid is thick and will help keep soap from going bad. It's extracted from rosemary leaves.

- Fragrance Fixers: Use 1 teaspoon in a 28 oz batch of soap

- Arrowroot-You'll want a powdered form; they do make flour with it that will work.

- Cornstarch-100% pure cornstarch works best, can be found in the grocery store.

- Oatmeal-You'll want to finely blend your oatmeal before adding it. Not only will this give your soap a light exfoliator it will help hold on to the scents you add.

- Orris Root-You'll want the powdered form; it's made from the dried and powdered root of an Iris. It has its own scent, woodsy and violet, so watch how it affects your soap, as you may not like it.

- Benzoin-Comes in a powder or essential oil and both will work.

- Soap Colors: Different ingredients we place in our soaps can impart different colors; Oils and fats can add yellowish hues to our soaps while we can use flowers, herbs and other natural ingredients even minerals to impart different colors into our soap naturally.

- Oils-Depending on the color of your oil will depend what color it gives your soap. Something like olive oil will give you a warm, creamy yellow color while the more white oil is the more white your soap will be.

- Clays-The colors we can get from clay are limited to the colors we find in the earth, but clays in powdered form can add nice color to your soap, as well as having detoxing properties and can add a light exfoliator.

- Minerals/Micas-These powders come in a wide variety of colors but you have to be careful if you're buying instead of making them, many are created and can still have added ingredients that are conducive to soap making and especially not organic soap.

- Herbs, Roots, Flowers-For this group you can really get creative, you can go with the obvious ingredients using ground up flowers and plants, but you can also use things like spinach to get a nice green color. So get creative grind it up and see what works for you. You can also buy powdered forms of many plants, etc., just check your labels, they are a very natural way to add color to your soap.

- Sugars-If you add milk, sugar or honey to your mixture before it reaches trace it will caramelize and can add some really nice color.

- Natural Botanicals: When I say botanicals I mean all the different parts of a plant or flower are considered a botanical. These can add a lot of interest to your soap, whether to give it a good overall visual effect, or for exfoliation purposes. There is some debate as to how much of the actual ingredients are left after going through the soap making process, so you'll have to use your own judgment on that. All herbal products must be in the dried form, not the fresh. If they are fresh they will turn dry and rot. Use ¼ cup per batch of soap, to start. After you have been making batches you will be able to determine the amount that pleases you most. Chamomile and lemongrass are both delicious smelling soap additives that can be grown at home and inexpensive.

- Botanical Oils-These are best when used in the superfatting stage, heat can cause a lot of the properties of the botanical to be lost so you'll have to use your own judgement. Make sure you notice if you are using essential oils, or blended artificial oil. It will make a difference in the amount of oil you need to add for scent. If they are essential oils, one measured teaspoon is the appropriate amount for a batch this size. If they are artificial, you should begin by doubling that amount.

- Dried Fruit and Spices-For these I like to use whole pieces for visual interest, or powdered forms of items for color and as an exfoliant. You can add a lemon slice to your soap to create an interesting visual effect, as well as to let the soap soak up its juicy goodness. Maybe you'll add a cinnamon stick to your soap for the nice effect, or powdered as an exfoliant and to give it color. The addition of powdered chlorophyll makes a brilliant green soap, turmeric makes a deep yellow orange, and cocoa powder makes a deep brown and a nice chocolate scent. Cocoa powder and essential peppermint oil make lovely chocolate mint gourmet soap. Cake food colorings does not hold up in soap, so these should be avoided.

- Exfoliants-There are lots you can use to add a nice exfoliant to your soap and give it great scrubbing power, so get creative. You can use things like ground up nuts, almonds are great and can add some of their oils to soap as well, ground pumice, and rolled oats are good additives. You'll want to use small amounts of the pumice and oats or you can overdo it with this scrubbers.

- Roots-There are lots of different roots, and many have different medicinal uses, but once again, because they are heated during our soap making process you risk losing those properties. They are also great at coloring your soap as well.

- Herbs and Flowers-These can give you a wide variety of decorative options as well as tints. If you want to use an infusion of flowers you should use it in place of the water you add. So if you have X cups of water and you want to use a quarter cup of infusion you'll substitute that quarter cup of water. You can also add petals to your soap as well, but they can lose their color during the soap making process. Also note the flowers can turn brown if not properly treated.

** Please note these ingredients should be in either a powder or liquid form to best suit the uses of soap making. These forms allow for best infusion and absorption into the soap itself.

We have touched on many basic concepts with soap making. A note of caution: remember the more natural you go with your ingredients the more natural your soap will be. If you want to go organic with your soap you'll need to pay attention to the different products you get, as long as you make sure your ingredients are classified as organic, you will have organic soap.

There are so many ways to make soap that it would take a much larger book to list all the methods. Besides cold process, which is what we covered in this book, there is also hot process. You can even make your soap in a crockpot.

I wish you luck on your soap making journey! Don't give up if your first few batches don't come out right, it may take a few tries so don't be discouraged. The perfect soap recipe combination is like making the first cake of the first batch of cement. You learn to eyeball the correct thickness, texture and consistency.

## CONCLUSION

**Thank you again for** downloading this book, Soap Making: Beginners Guide to Making Natural Herbal Handmade Organic Soaps from Scratch!

I hope this book was able to help you to learn which products to purchase to make your first batch of natural herbal handmade organic soap.

The next step is to gather the utensils, the ingredients, the safety equipment, and a well ventilated room, and jump into the handmade soap making hobby. If you enjoy it and practice it enough, it might turn into a lucrative side business with a wonderful product that sells itself.

Finally, if you enjoyed this book, please take the time to share your thoughts and post a review on Amazon. It'd be greatly appreciated!

Thank you and good luck!

Preview Of **"MUDRAS: *The Simple Beginners Guide To Using Hand Gestures For Healing, Weight Loss, Yoga And Chakras*"** By Laurent Wygant

# PRACTICING THE MUDRAS

Now that you have learned the basics of Mudras and what it is time to learn how to practice them. The following is a list of the most commonly used Mudras and how each individual Mudra benefits different parts and functions of your body and mind.

Gyan Mudra: Knowledge

How to: Touch the tips of your index finger and thumb together, while stretching out the remaining three fingers.

The tip of the thumb connects to the pituitary gland and endocrine gland. Pressing the thumb and index finger together, allows these glands to be active. The benefits of Gyan Mudra are that it prevents and cures insomnia, and increases memory and concentration. It relieves stress, anger, anxiety and depression when regularly practiced.

Prithvi Mudra: Earth

How to: Touch your thumb and the tip of your ring together, while stretching out the remaining three fingers.

By pressing the tips of these two fingers together, you are increasing physical strength. The benefits of Prithvi Mudra include healthier and clearer skin and improved body functions. It improves your blood flow and circulation and boosts your concentration and focus. It also helps to heal back pains, joint pains, and arthritis.

Kashyapa Mudra

How to: Make your hand into a fist and allow your thumb to stick out in between your middle and ring fingers.

Practicing the Kashyapa Mudra represents balance and also helps to protect you from negative energies.

Surahi Mudra

How to: Press your little finger on the ring finger of the opposite hand and repeat with the other hand.

Practicing the Surahi Mudra is known to improve and sharpen your intellect, as well as prevent and cure colds, respiratory problems, and rheumatic problems.

Apana Mudra: Detox

How to: Touch the tips of your middle finger and ring finger to the tip of your thumb, while extending the remaining two fingers.

The body releases carbon dioxide through all of its bodily functions. Practicing the Apana Mudra increases and accelerates those releases. This improves your skin and eyes. It can also clear up respiratory problems and increase your confidence and patience.

Ganesha Mudra

How to: Hold your right palm in front of your chest, facing your chest. With your left hand, firmly grasp the fingers of your right hand. Your elbows should be pointed out to your sides.

It is best to practice the Ganesha Mudra whenever you are facing troubles or obstacles in your life. In Hindu mythology, Ganesha was the "Elephant God." His role is to remove the problems that are in your life and give you the will and energy to persevere when you feel as if you cannot make it through. It will also relieve tension in your chest, shoulders, and arms.

Varuna Mudra: Water

How to: Touch the tips of your little finger and thumb together, while stretching the other three out. It is often practiced when sitting, standing or lying down.

Practicing the Varuna Mudra freshens the body and prevents diseases that are caused by dehydration and lack of water. It cures dryness and other skin issues, as well as adding a glow to your skin. It also benefits your blood flow and helps to cure urinary ailments.

## Vayu Mudra: Air

How to: Touch the index finger to the base of your thumb, while stretching out the remaining three fingers. Some of the benefits of practicing the Vayu Mudra include the relief of many diseases such as arthritis, Parkinson's disease, and other rheumatic aliments. It also relieves gastrointestinal distress.

**Note: This Mudra should only be practiced until your ailment is cured.

## Uttarabodhi Mudra

How to: Press together your index fingers and keep them pointed up. Press together your thumb and keep them pointing down. Interlock your remaining fingers and hold this Mudra in front of your abdomen, or Solar Plexus.

Practice the Uttarabodhi Mudra when you are feeling drained or are about to do an activity that requires a lot of energy. This Mudra will help boost your energy and essentially recharge your body.

## Aakaash Mudra (Aakaas-vardhak Mudra)

How to: Touch the tip of your thumb to the tip of your middle finger and extend the remaining fingers.

The Aakaash Mudra is often known as the "Space Mudra" or "Ether Mudra." It replaces the negative thoughts and emotions, with positive thoughts and emotions. Practicing the Aakaash Mudra also improves your intuition and it helps to relieve colds and congestion, ear infections, and high blood pressure. Practice the Aakaash Mudra if you are feeling nauseas or have motion sickness.

Anjali Mudra

How to: Touch your palms together in front of your heart. This mudra is used to express respect, gratitude, and love. This is often used when mediating and ending prayer in yoga. "Anjali Mudra" actually means "Namaste," which is commonly used when practicing yoga. This Mudra is also cures anxiety and stress and allows for a deep spiritual connection during meditation and practice.

Vajra Mudra

How to: Touch the tips of your middle finger, ring finger, and little finger to the tip of your thumb, while keeping your index finger extended.

This Mudra represents a lightning bolt, as well as all five elements. Practicing the Vajra Mudra increases blood flow and helps to lower your intake of coffee, tobacco, and other habits. It also sharpens your intellect and concentration.

Agni Mudra: Fire

How to: Fold your ring finger over your palm and cover it with your thumb. This is practiced while in a sitting position.

Practicing the Agni Mudra boosts your metabolism and improves digestion and cholesterol levels. It also helps to eliminate anxiety and stress. Agni Mudra is known to reduce and prevent respiratory and heart ailments. Regularly practicing Agni can also strengthen your vision.

Shunya Mudra: Emptiness

How to: Keep the middle finger on the base of the thumb and cover the middle finger with the thumb. Keep the remaining three fingers straight. Practicing the Shunya Mudra will relieve an ear ache in about five minutes. It is also known to relieve all other ear issues such as, ringing in the ears and other hearing problems.

**Note: This Mudra should only be practiced until your ailment is cured.

Lotus Mudra

How to: Connect your thumbs and little fingers together, as well as your palms. Open and stretch your remaining fingers out like a flower and hold in front of your chest.

Practicing the Lotus Mudra is excellent for your everyday mental health, especially when you are feeling lonely or drained. It is also helpful when you want to share affection and compassion with others. The Lotus Mudra represents purity and encourages you to recognize the beauty in you, as well as the beauty in the people that surround you. The imagery of a blossoming flower that we create with our hands, reminds us to open our hearts.

### Tse Mudra

How to: Fold your thumb over your palm and cover it with the remaining fingers.

Practicing the Tse Mudra helps to relieve depression, stress and anxiety. It increases your intuition and can help to improve your bladder and kidney functions.

### Prana Mudra: Life

How to: Touch the tips of your ring finger and little finger to the tip of your thumb, keeping the other two fingers straight. Prana represents life and its energy. By practicing the Prana Mudra, you will be stronger and full of energy. It also boosts your immune system and improves your eyes. It can help to prevent or cure insomnia and significantly reduce anxiety and stress. Practice Prana Mudra to prevent hair loss as well. It also promotes hair regrowth.

### Surabhi Mudra

How to: Touch the tip of your little finger on your right hand to the tip of your index finger on your left hand. Touch the tip of your little finger on your left hand to the tip of your index finger on your right hand. Touch the tip of your index finger on your right hand to the tip of the middle finger on your left hand. Touch the tip of your index finger on your left hand to the tip of your middle finger on your right hand. Finally, the thumbs should be extended out.

Practicing the Surabhi Mudra is a little more advanced than most of the other Mudras, however it is very effective. This Mudra can help to heal arthritis and other rheumatic diseases. It also benefits your mind and improves hormonal balance.

Bhramara Mudra

How to: Press your index finger on the base of your thumb. Press the tip of your thumb on the side of your middle finger, just below the nail. Stretch out the remaining two fingers.In Sanskrit, Bhramara translates to "male bee." This Mudra is practiced to lessen existing allergy symptoms and to also prevent them. It also helps reduce sinus pressure and can break-up congestion in your lungs.

Saakat Mudra

How to: Touch together the tips of both of both of your thumb and both of your index fingers. While in a sitting position, point your thumbs toward your heart, with the index fingers pointed slightly down. Practicing Saakat Mudra will help you to lessen and control your temper. It is known to relieve mental pressure and tension and put your mind at ease.

Jal Shaamak Mudra

How to: Place the tip of your little finger to the base of your thumb, then cover your little finger with your thumb. Practice this Mudras if you are having troubles with excessive sweating, a runny nose, or watery eyes. The Jal Shaamak Mudra will also benefit you if you are having issues with retaining water.

**Mudras for Weight Loss**

There are several different Mudras you can practice to help lose weight, control your weight, and improve your digestive system.

- Linga Mudra: Heat

    How to: Interlock your fingers together while keeping your left thumb straight. Wrap your right thumb around the base of your left thumb. Practicing the Linga Mudra will help to generate heat throughout your body. The benefit of this Mudra is that helps with weight loss and provides chest cold relief, by helping to rid your lungs of phlegm. It also gives more power to your lungs and boosts your immune system. Linga Mudra can benefit and improve respiratory ailments, such as asthma.

    **Note: Do not continue to practice this Mudra once your ailments have been cured. Over practice of Linga Mudra may lead to laziness, fatigue, and lethargy.

- Surya Mudra: Sun

    How to: Keep the ring finger on the base of the thumb and cover the ring finger with your thumb, just below the nail. Stretch out the remaining fingers out. This hand gesture is connected to your thyroid gland and helps you to lose weight and improve digestion. It is also known to lower cholesterol levels, reduce anxiety and prevent heart-related ailments.

- <u>Vaayan Mudra</u>

    How to: Touch the tips of your index and middle finger to the tip of your thumb, while extending the remaining two fingers. There are many benefits of the Vaayan Mudra such as defeating lazy, drowsy, and lethargic feelings, as well as helping to prevent nervous breakdowns.

- <u>Kapha-naashak Mudra</u>

    How to: Touch your little finger and ring finger to the base of your thumb and gently cover those finger with your thumb. Extend the remaining fingers straight out. Practicing this Mudra will boost your metabolism and improve your digestive system.

End of this sample book.

Enjoyed the preview?

See details for this book in the Kindle Store or Simply search on Amazon.

Search for "Mudras by Laurent Wygant"

# Why Not Check Out Our Other Recommended Books

Below you'll find some other popular books that are on Amazon and Kindle as well.

Amazon Affiliate: Amazon Associates Program: The Ultimate Business Guide to Make Money Online By Shane Blanc

Amazon FBA: Learn The Secrets of Selling Physical & Private Labelled Products on Amazon By Shane Blanc

Bonsai: Bonsai Care: The Ultimate Guide To Bonsai Tree Care (Watering, Growing, Botanical, Home Gardening) By Henry Durden

Horseback Riding: Six Quick ways to Master your Equestrian & Equitation Skills in 30 Minutes By Declan Strauss & Laurent Wygant

Online Arbitrage: How to Steps To Make Money Online From Sourcing and Selling Products On Amazon By Shane Blanc

Shyness: The Ultimate Guide to Overcoming Social Anxiety & being Shy By Laurent Wygant

You can simply search for these titles on the Amazon website to find them.

Made in the USA
Middletown, DE
19 December 2016